Keeping *Fresh* When You're Frantic

D1570810

Keeping *Fresh* When You're Frantic

Renewing your spiritual life

PRESENTED BY

Jill Briscoe

NexGen™ is an imprint of
Cook Communications Ministries, Colorado Springs, Colorado 80918
Cook Communications, Paris, Ontario
Kingsway Communications, Eastbourne, England

KEEPING FRESH WHEN YOU'RE FRANTIC
© 2003 by *Just Between Us* magazine

First Printing, 2003
Printed in the United States of America

1 2 3 4 5 6 7 8 9 10 Printing/Year 07 06 05 04 03

This book is part of a series on relevant issues for today's Christian woman.
For more information on other titles in this series or for information about *Just Between Us* magazine, please turn to the back of this book.

Unless otherwise noted, Scripture quotations are taken from the Holy Bible: New International Version®. Copyright © 1973, 1978, 1984 by International Bible Society. Used by permission of Zondervan Publishing House. All rights reserved. Scripture quotations marked (NASB) are taken from the NEW AMERICAN STANDARD BIBLE®, Copyright The Lockman Foundation 1960, 1962, 1963, 1968, 1971, 1972, 1973, 1975, 1977, 1995. Used by permission.

Library of Congress Cataloging-in-Publication Data

Keeping fresh when you're frantic : renewing your spiritual life / [edited by] Jill Briscoe.
        p. cm. -- (Just between us)
    ISBN 0-7814-3956-6 (booklet : pbk.)
    1. Christian women--Religious life. I. Briscoe, Jill. II. Series.
    BV4527.K44213 2003
    248.8'43--dc21
                                    2003006902

contents

A Note from Jill Briscoe

Dear Friends,

We can all relate to the ongoing need for renewal in the midst of our busy day. However, we are seemingly on the run from early morning till late at night and can't seem to find the precious minutes to *be still*. Over and over again women tell me what an ongoing struggle this is for them. I quite understand. It's an ongoing struggle for me too!

In Luke 10 we meet Martha who was seemingly too busy to be blessed. Jesus did not rebuke her busyness but rather her anxiety about it. He would take our worry about our work away from us, relieving us of the stress that is so often the straw that breaks the camel's back. Martha's problem is so often ours. We are *distracted by our much serving* and become as someone has said *more concerned with the work of the Lord than the Lord of the work!* It is so easy to do.

There was nothing wrong with Martha's love and devotion for Jesus. But busyness that hustles out to meet the day without meeting Jesus first, is busyness that will soon be busy bossing everyone around, getting irritated, self-righteous, and downright hostile with everyone in sight. What is more, it is an activity that will end up in an accusing, *Lord, don't you care that my sister has left me to do the work by myself? Tell her to help me!* (Luke 10:40)

Of course He cares! He would have us join Mary at His feet so He can tell us how much He cares. You might be tempted to think it was easy for Mary. She was obviously of a very different temperament than her sister. But we must be careful; we must not presume we really know what Mary's temperament was like. Some commentators point out that Jesus said she had *chosen* the better part. If this was the case, they suggest, perhaps she was *Martha before she was Mary.* That's a neat thought. Maybe Mary was even more of a Martha than Martha! The point is, whatever our temperament or inclination to worship, we *all* need to make a daily choice to meet Him some time, some place that fits our particular schedule. If we do, we will go out to serve with His blessing resting on our service, His peace in our hearts, His joy on our lips. If we don't take time to be renewed, we'll end up receiving a well-earned rebuke at the end of the day!

So come ye apart and rest awhile—as Jesus invited you. If you don't, you may well find yourself coming apart!

May I Offer Some Practical Ideas?

1. Take your calendar off the wall and find the *best* time (it will probably be different each day) to meet with the Lord. Write it on your schedule and then keep your appointment.

2. Start with fifteen minutes a day (don't be overly ambitious).

3. Have a plan. Select a short portion of Scripture as something to remember and write it down in a notebook. Record written prayer requests—if you don't know where to start, try the Epistles— Philippians maybe.

4. "Be still" and know that He is God—sometime during this exercise.

5. Be faithful—and if you are, you will be blessed. Then it follows, if you are blessed, you will be bound to be a blessing!

Finally, take some of the various suggestions throughout this book and implement them into your own time with God; you might just discover how your relationship with God and life can become freshened instead of frantic!

In His Joy,

Jill Briscoe

chapter one

Renewal
on the Run

Jill Briscoe

*H*ere's a sobering statistic: 40 percent of ministry wives never have a quiet time. Why? For many reasons. But one of the reasons will be *they never have*. They don't know how. And now that they're ministry wives, who are they going to ask?

The more involved we get in the ministry, the harder it is to ask some elementary questions. "I was raised in a Christian home and they presumed I knew all these things," a girl married to a parachurch worker said to me. "But I don't know how to dig deeper on my own. I don't know how to get a message from the Bible to give to someone else. I don't even know how to put together a little five-minute devotional. Nobody's ever told me that, taught me that. And what's more, I don't know how to get answers from the Bible to my own heart questions."

This is where humility comes in. That ministry wife had the beautiful quality of humility that enabled her to admit her need. Let's be "small enough to be big enough" to ask for help! A very well-known preacher, when he left seminary, made a list of twenty men he admired. He wrote to them all and said, "I want to learn the secret of your effectiveness. If I get myself to where you are (and they were all over the United States), would you give me one hour of your time?"

That's an example of humility with a purpose. Can you imagine any of those men turning down an offer like that? With that kind of hunger to learn?

So put away the notion that you should have figured out all of this information magically over the years, that it was supposed to float down from heaven and descend upon you when your husband and/or you got ordained or commissioned for special service. It doesn't happen like that. As Jesus said, "Ask and it will be given to you; seek and you will find; knock and the door will be opened to you" (Matt. 7:7).

Losing Our Cutting Edge

How easy it is to lose the *cutting edge* of our Christian life—even when we are living in a Christian environment. There was a young man in a school for believers who did just that. The principal of the school was Elijah, and enrollment was so healthy that expansion was planned. All the students set to work to help.

There was one young man who borrowed an ax (a very precious implement in those days) and set about felling trees to clear a plot of ground by a river for the new buildings. He went to his task with great enthusiasm, but suddenly the ax head flew off the handle and fell into the river. He had lost his *cutting edge*.

"Oh Master," he cried to Elijah, "it was borrowed." Elijah took a piece of wood, threw it into the river, and the ax head floated to the top.

At different times in our lives we lose our cutting edge for one reason or another. In my own experience, I have found my life singularly ineffective for many reasons. For instance, it has been easy to rely on Jesus' friends instead of on my friend Jesus. I love to work for the Lord but can become so absorbed that the Lord of my work comes last on my agenda! The quiet time fades into the background. The prayers grow sporadic. Lack of time in God's presence leads to a lack of trust in His promises. Lack of trust soon translates into lack of power, and fear instead of faith has left me clutching an "ax handle" with no potential at all.

I have also discovered that I need to apply a piece of wood shaped like a cross to my helplessness at these times to bring the sharpness back to my Christian life and witness. Christ died to make me fit for heaven but lives to a make me fit for earth. As surely as His death brings life to my soul, His life brings a razor-sharp impact to my daily doings. It is up to me, however, to put out my hand and appropriate the cutting edge as He brings it within my reach again.

Whenever you become conscious that you are "blunt" ask yourself, "Where did I lose my edge?" Like the young man in the story, go back to that place and express to your heavenly Elijah (Jesus Christ) your sorrow and repentance for losing such a precious thing. He will make the iron float if you ask Him. Ask the Lord to help you do whatever it takes to get that edge back where it belongs. "Blunt" believers will never accomplish the work the Lord wants done. They will only succeed in damaging everyone around them and bringing grief to the Savior's heart.

That cutting edge is a matter of grace; it is a gift from God. And we receive gifts when we are in His presence. The devotional time you spend with the Lord not only sustains you through the trials and triumphs of being a ministry wife, but it makes the difference between you being effective or ineffective.

Bible Study

I'm going to say very little here. Again, there are tons of materials out there to help you study your Bible. Just don't let anything get in the way of letting God's Word change you.

A constant temptation with Bible study (and with prayer) is to give up when you've tried a system and couldn't get consistent with it. So you reorganize, choose an entirely new system, buy a new notebook, start at a different passage, and fail again in a few weeks. Satan loves to see us discouraged. So start with fifteen minutes. Read anything in the Word you want. When you fall, pick yourself up again. Throw away the system if it becomes too burdensome. So what if you're already behind a month in your "read-the-Bible-in-a-year" program? Just go back to being there every day, with the Lord, in His Word, asking the important questions: "What part of this Scripture is for me? What part of Your work is *my* work today? What sins do I need to confess? What is holding me back? What principle can help me in this area? What encouraging truth should I remember?"

There is a wise saying: *God doesn't call us to be successful; He calls us to be faithful.* Every time you come back to the Word, every time you attempt again to "be still" and know Him, that is counted to you as faithfulness in the Lord's eyes. And He will tell you what you need to know.

Prayer

Prayer is communication with God. Sometimes prayer is talking to God, telling Him your struggles, your pains, your anxieties—or your joys. God becomes the confidante, the friend who will understand perfectly and love completely.

Sometimes prayer is listening to God. Maybe with the Bible open on your lap. Maybe in the silence of your living room in between kids and neighbors and housework or while feeding a newborn baby. Most of us are not good listeners; we need more practice at this part of prayer.

> ### LifeLifters
> "*No* one graduates from Bible study until he meets its author face to face."
> —**Everett Haires**—

And sometimes, prayer is something that cannot be heard or uttered. The Bible says that the Holy Spirit prays for us when we can't pray for ourselves. When all we have inside us is a huge sigh of discouragement, then just be still and sigh! Then think about Him praying for you about it. Sometimes we cannot pray in the forms that have always been expected and acceptable. We can be as honest as we like, transparent before the Lord, and we won't be rejected. If all we have to offer is a groan or a scream, that is a prayer He'll gladly interpret and answer. When we are in severe emotional pain, it may be virtually impossible for us to have the emotional coherence to pray a "coherent" prayer. We may not have a single "nice" thing to say to God. Maybe all we can say is "Help!" or, "You hurt me!" Maybe all we can utter is the name of Jesus. And that's all right. Utter it!

The Holy Spirit has a job to do. He has many functions, actually, and one of them is to translate our prayers to the Father. He takes our groans, our screams, our tears, our muddled phrases, and He transforms them into pure offerings. Prayer opens those lines of heart communication to God Almighty. What a release. Unless we learn to grow in the dimension of our prayer life we will never survive, or revive the ministry.

Pray however you can, whenever you can, wherever you can. Pray in the morning and pray in the evening. Pray through the night. Pray in the kitchen and pray in the car. Pray in the chaos and pray in the order. Pray at the high points and pray at the low points. Pray when you can and pray when you can't. Prayer is your lifeline!

A person who relies upon God and listens for His voice is in prayer constantly, her heart open and waiting, her questions, her praises, her problems, all placed before God almost instantaneously, as naturally as breathing.

Don't give up praying. And if you have to start again, give God whatever you've got! It will change your life. It won't only renew your spiritual life; it will bring reality into your ministry.

Reprinted from Renewal on the Run: Encouragement for Wives Who are Partners in Ministry, *(© 1992, by Jill Briscoe. Used by permission of Harold Shaw Publishers, Wheaton, IL.)*

... and Shut the *Door*

Lonnie Collins Pratt

*F*ew Christians doubt the value of spending time alone with God. Books and articles abound that urge us to schedule a daily "quiet time" of prayer, Bible reading, and meditation on God's truths.

But while wrestling with difficult dilemmas and doubts during a mid-life crisis, I considered taking an extended "personal retreat" to make more time to be alone with the Lord.

At first, the idea seemed too radical and selfish. But my situation almost compelled me to get away from my normal routine for a few days.

That was my first period of extended solitude—but it was not my last. As part of my spiritual discipline, I now get out of my office and routine at least one day every two months, and every year I plan two or three "retreats" of at least two days.

As I studied the Bible, I found that this habit was one Jesus Himself practiced and encouraged. He frequently slipped away from the crowd to be alone with His Father. And when teaching His disciples about prayer, He instructed them to be alone, to "shut the door" (Matt. 6:6, NASB).

Still, modern Christians are unaccustomed to spending long periods of time alone. As I told some of my friends about my experience, I noticed they often raised the same kinds of concerns. I'd like to answer some of these worries—and then go on to point out some of the positive benefits of solitude. Perhaps you will find a place in your year for such times.

"I don't think I could find anything to do for more than a couple of hours. Doesn't it get boring?"

These days, most of us have been conditioned to be entertained and occupied every waking moment. It seems impossible that solitude would be anything but boring. Western culture has taught us to accept noise and crowds. How many people do you know who turn on the television or radio when they're alone, "just for background noise?"

But there is a time to be still before God. Quieting ourselves means wrestling with our urge to go out and do something.

"The whole idea sounds sort of mystical and New Age-ish to me."

Jesus Himself withdrew frequently into solitude. His ministry was launched after being alone for forty days (Matt. 4:1-11). After feeding five thousand, He headed for solitude (Matt. 14:23).

He instructed His disciples to do the same. After they returned from ministering, He told them, "Come with me by yourselves to a quiet place and get some rest" (Mark 6:30-31).

New Age religions have adapted various Christian

concepts to their own heresy, but this doesn't nullify the value of solitude with God.

"Strong Christians don't need solitude. If you just lean on God, you don't need to go hide out in the woods. Strong people shouldn't try to escape."

Too often we think of those who cherish solitude as indulging themselves in selfish escapism from the real world—but the opposite is true.

Once more, Jesus is the best example of this. The forty days in the wilderness were a time of strengthening and preparation for Him, as He proved when He powerfully dealt with the tempter.

Before choosing disciples, before facing Calvary, before revealing Himself as Messiah, Jesus entered solitude. Jesus used the discipline of solitude to *face* reality, not hide from it.

"It seems so self-centered. How can considerate people leave their job, children, spouse, and responsibilities on a whim?"

When we abstain from human relationships, denying ourselves their support and companionship, we pull away from everything that demands our conformity in a fallen world. Rather than creating a disdain for people, solitude forms a dependence on God, which always breeds love for others.

The Benefits of Solitude

Solitude forces us to realize our dependence on God.

In the safety of our relationships and the satisfaction of our work, we tend to forget who really matters. "They remembered that God was their Rock" (Ps. 78:35). Scripture tells us that solitude is one way to heed God's call to remember (Ps. 77:3-12; 103:17-18).

By isolating ourselves for a while from other dependencies, we lean harder on God; we follow harder after Him.

Solitude allows us to sort out the teachings of the Bible for ourselves.

One of my own driving questions has been: *Does God possess me, or do my ideas about God possess me?* None of us approach God or the Bible without preconceived ideas about who God is and what Scripture must say.

These prejudices are hard for us to spot if everyone in our sphere of influence—preacher, spouse, teacher—confirms our bias. For example, until I began practicing solitude I never had an original thought about the second coming of Jesus. I merely echoed my minister's and college professors'. Spending time alone with God and His Word, allowed me to discover fresh insights.

Solitude provides an opportunity for rest, both physical and mental.

Rest was instituted by God in the Sabbath. But few of us hold one day a week strictly as a day of rest. All of creation—including human beings—need rest.

For those who feel guilty when they take a nap, solitude provides an opportunity to rest our bodies and free our minds of influences that are actually hostile to God. By pulling away from these influences, we give our minds peace and freedom to receive and hear God.

Solitude gives a chance to "dream dreams" for our lives.

Alone with God is the safest place any of us will ever be. This is where we can evaluate the direction and purpose of our lives. This is where we can dare to whisper the dreams we seldom share.

Long Periods of Solitude

A personal retreat is a decision to be alone for an extended period.

In Sue Monk Kidd's book, *God's Joyful Surprise,* we read: "A withdrawal for quiet attentiveness to God without structure or program was, well ... unusual. I pondered whether anyone would condone anything so solitary and 'inward' as this. It had always seemed safer and more acceptable to get to work ... Most of us spend our lives running from the moment when the noise stops and we are alone in the silence. For there we come to the end of ourselves and arrive at the truth that reaches to the underside of our soul—that we are all, ultimately, alone. And in the end we must find the music of God alone, within ourselves."

I've found a few guidelines help me focus on God during times of planned solitude. Don't drag along a pile of books, records, tapes, or other "accessories." Bring your Bible and a notebook. If there is a book that has been especially helpful to you in your Christian walk, bring it too. (I like to reread works by C. S. Lewis, Joseph Bayly, and Frederick Buechner.)

Pick the site carefully. Water has a calming effect on me, so I try to go to a lake. Campgrounds, retreat centers, and borrowed cottages are plentiful and cheap. You don't need to spend a lot of money to find a suitable place.

Keep meals simple. Fruit, vegetables, and bread are good choices. Don't spend your time cooking.

Bring comfortable clothing and walking shoes. If you're near water, throw in your swimsuit. Get exercise. Swimming and walking are good choices. When I'm alone, I need more exercise than usual to keep my thinking clear.

Depending on your retreat location, you might want to bring insect repellent and sunscreen too. Leave makeup, razors, hair dryers, and the like at home. You'll want soap and towels, but try to cut your morning routine to the barest elements.

Don't schedule your time rigidly. While it's good to plan for the retreat, avoid detailed scheduling of daily activities. If you tie yourself to an agenda and a list of "must-do" tasks, the experience is far less refreshing.

> ### LifeLifters
>
> "*If* the Christian is too busy to stop, take spiritual inventory, and receive his assignments from God, he becomes a slave to the tyranny of the urgent. He may work day and night to achieve much that seems significant to himself and others, but he will not finish the work God has for him to do."
>
> —**Charles E. Hummel**—

If you must have a routine, keep it in general terms. For example, maybe you'd like to pray before breakfast and take a walk each evening. Or you might plan to read an entire chapter in Scripture. You'll need time for journal notes too. Be flexible. If you cram activities—even spiritual activities—into each minute, you might feel guilty if you stare at the lake for three hours. But maybe what you actually need are a few hours of staring at the lake.

Short Intervals of Solitude

It isn't always possible to drop everything and go off alone. It's also important to maintain the peace of God day by day.

Since many Christians have established prayer and devotional times, perhaps you could consider extending this period by fifteen minutes. Shut your eyes and pick a favorite psalm, verse, or hymn to focus on. Just sit quietly, breath deeply, and, in the words of Psalm 46, be still.

Our desire for time alone with God is a response to God's overwhelming love for us. The late Malcolm Muggeridge wrote, "I have never wanted a God or feared a God, or felt the necessity to invent one. Unfortunately, I am driven to the conclusion that God wants me. God comes padding after me like a Hound of Heaven."

For me, it is when I am alone that I stop scurrying away from the sound of God's pursuit. Instead, I let Him in and shut the door.

chapter three

The Top 10
Stumbling Blocks
to Personal Devotions

Ingrid Lawrenz, MSW

1. My housework must be done before I "take time for myself."

Housework will never be completely finished; there will always be more to do or someone will eat something and create "dishes and crumbs."

2. My devotional time must always be long and the study intense to be effective.

Small regular meals with God can keep you connected to your Father.

3. Devotions must be a time of suffering. If I have a cup of coffee or do them while I relax on my patio, it doesn't count.

Time with God is meant to be a time of refreshment—like a deer drinking the fresh water it was panting for.

4. My kids constantly disturb me.

If they want your attention, you can bring them into your study time by praying aloud with them and by telling them the Bible story you're reading, at a level they can easily understand.

5. My husband, as the spiritual leader of the family, must lead me into it.

Great if he does, but if he's gone too much or spiritually running on empty himself, he needs your prayers more than ever and he will greatly benefit from your spiritual strength.

6. I'm too unworthy to approach God. He doesn't want to be bothered by me.

Christ bore our shame on the cross. He is the one constantly safe person in our lives who will always welcome us warmly.

7. I haven't done enough praying or studying lately, so I'll only feel too ashamed to come before God now, with just a little time for devotions.

Confess your negligence. God is always happy to hear from one of His precious children. The Bible says, pray constantly. Sometimes those short sentence prayers sent up throughout the day in every situation, help you to keep your heart fixed on Jesus.

8. I'm neither an early robin or a late owl, so I just can't seem to find the time.

Doctors say our bodies run in constant rhythms, bedtime and waking cycles, but also ninety-minute swells and ebbs of energy throughout the day. In the middle of the afternoon, you can expect your body to want a rest time also. Doctors say it does our bodies well to listen to our rhythms. We stay healthier this way. God is waiting at any of our resting times, for a "quiet time" of refreshment with Him.

9. I'm too depressed to read or pray.

It's at times like these that the Holy Spirit can pray for us through our literal "groans." Short, concrete prayers are fine also. It's the seeking of the relationship, of connecting with God, that's important—even at times when we feel disconnected from everyone and everything. Seeking out Bible passages on comfort is more helpful at times like these than rigid, methodical "so many verses" reading.

10. I have trouble praying because my mind wanders too much.

Journal praying can be most helpful for this problem. Writing in prayer form can help you corral your thoughts before God. Going down a written prayer list can also help you keep on track.

chapter four

Rekindling Your First Love

Find out how you can keep
your love for Christ first.

Shelly Esser

Today, among many Christian women, there is a growing sense that spiritual intimacy and renewal come from involvement in more and more activities. We somehow conclude that God is happiest with us when our schedules, our relationships, and our ministries are packed full.

If the truth were known, however, many of us would have to admit that while our schedules are bulging, we're enjoying life less. At the very center of our quest for deeper intimacy with Christ there is a nagging emptiness, a dullness, a distance, a joylessness, that penetrates our inner spirits. We wonder how we got here. Perhaps the greatest challenge facing us today as Christian women is to keep first things first—to keep our love for Christ passionate and alive. That will mean making a deliberate effort every day to put Christ as our top priority, which will often mean some conscious rearranging of our priorities.

I've often struggled with this in my own life and have had to seriously examine myself recognizing the desperate condition of my own heart—facing the reality that I can so easily suffer from *heart trouble.*

The Church of Ephesus in Revelation 2:1-4 was another group of believers who experienced severe *heart trouble*—the kind of heart trouble that threatened their love life with Jesus. They were church people like you and me who made the mistake of getting caught up in the busyness of the ministry, losing sight of the purpose in the process. From all appearances, they looked like the perfect church—committed, dedicated, good Christians, living for Christ, or so they thought. However, Jesus looked into their hearts and came up with a very different diagnosis. I wonder if He were to look into our hearts what diagnosis He would have for us?

In verse 4, Jesus harshly rebukes this busy little church, "Yet I hold this against you: You have forsaken your first love." This busy, separated, sacrificing church had *abandoned* or *left* their first love, replacing it with sound doctrine and busy activity—not bad things in themselves. Sure, these believers were involved in ministering for Christ, but they carelessly put all of their emphasis on service at the expense of their deep devotion to Christ. They had reached the place in their lives of all output with no input, and if we're not careful, we can make the same mistake.

Have you ever noticed how busyness has become a way of life in our society—and, now, even in the church? It's almost an addiction. We often think that the busier we are, the more spiritual we are. As the

Church of Ephesus exemplifies, that is simply not true. Jesus wants our hearts, not just our hands and heads. Wesley L. Duewel, in his book, *Ablaze for God,* says, "The most crucial danger to a leader is to be so busy as to neglect to love Jesus, to fail to live a life of ardent devotion and 'in-loveness' to Jesus."

Christian service is a poor substitute for Jesus Himself. We need to ask ourselves, "Do I want to run myself into the ground doing things for God, or do I want the best part—knowing Him and loving Him face to face? Yes, service is very important, but not apart from the One whom we serve. If our focus is only on ministry rather than our walk with Christ, we will never truly put Him first.

There must be a balance, of course, but more often than not we err on the side of busyness. Millie Dienert once said, "Any activity we involve ourselves in that is not directed by the Holy Spirit is just a bunch of busyness." How true. Sadly, we get to the places in our lives and ministries where our activities become passionless, even Christless. We need to be careful that we do not become *busied out of* or *hurried out of* our relationship with Christ, as Gigi Graham Tchividjian says in her book, *A Woman's Quest for Serenity.* Christian living is living in love with Jesus! Daily, we must choose to love Jesus.

How do we know when we've lost our First Love? I believe it begins when we lose our sense of needing Christ. When you think about it, it's our need for Christ in the first place that is the very motivation for our salvation. But often, once God begins to meet the needs in our lives, we tend to forget we still have them, don't we? We become self-sufficient and self-absorbed. I'm sure those in the Church of Ephesus were running the church quite efficiently. They knew how to implement all the right programs. They knew all of the latest techniques and formulas for ministry. However, they left out the Lord in the process. They became busy *for* God not busy *with* God, and there is a big difference. What we are in public stems from what we are in private.

Whether we realize it or not, we are always in deep, acute need of Jesus Christ in our lives. We are in danger of losing our First Love when we don't recognize the continual depth of our need. That's why praise is so important in the Christian life. It keeps us aware that everything we have in life only comes through God's loving and gracious hand.

> ### Life Lifters
>
> "*We* can accept the reality of limitation. The truth is that we can neither respond to every need nor accept every invitation. So the practical question is not whether we will draw the line, but where we will draw the line."
>
> —**Howard R. Macy**—

Perhaps you haven't fallen into the busyness trap like the Ephesians did, but there are many other traps that have the potential to give us heart trouble: possessions, success, relationships—to name a few. God did not create us to find satisfaction in things—not even in ministry. He created us to find complete satisfaction in Him. Did you know that fear of loss is often God's first signal to us that we have transferred our dependence from Him onto something or someone else? What are you holding on to today? What's giving you heart trouble?

Are you willing to let it go so you can be a First-Love Christian? We often wonder why we're so weary, always running on empty. Only Jesus can satisfy. Only He can keep us from heart trouble.

Well, this could all get pretty discouraging and hopeless, but we need to go back to our text. In verse 5 we discover that Christ doesn't just rebuke the believers there; He goes on to give them a prescription for their heart trouble: "Remember the height from which you have fallen! Repent and do the things you did at first." The Ephesians were first "to keep on remembering" the height from which they had fallen.

What does that mean? These believers had once enjoyed a close relationship with God; they were to go back and remember and recall that time. We must never forget what Christ has saved us from. We need to remember the depth of His grace, and forgiveness in our lives—we need to always remember the cross. Have you lost the thrill of knowing Christ? Then go back and remember what it was that caused you to fall in love with Him in the beginning. Think about those first days as a new believer.

Secondly, to rekindle our First Love we are to repent. This means changing our attitudes and affections. Like the Ephesians, we will need to turn away from our coldness and our indifference, and return once again to a vital relationship with Christ. Likewise, we need to realize our own sinfulness and susceptibility to let other things—good things—take first place in our lives. Jeremiah 17:9 says, "The heart is deceitful above all things." We need to know our own hearts well and the competitors that reside there.

At the first indication of heart trouble, we need to repent and pray for God's power to keep Him first. When our hearts are truly focused on Christ, the world can never steal our love for Him away.

This will mean regular time in God's Word and prayer so the Holy Spirit can condition our hearts to love Christ first. Susanna Wesley told her children that anything that dulled their desire for God was sin for them. Each of us must regularly assess our own lives and develop an awareness to the areas that can easily hinder our love for Christ. Having regular "First-Love checks" can help us keep Christ first.

The last part of the prescription is a warning to *read the label carefully*. Jesus told the church that He would "remove the lampstand from its place." In other words, the church would cease to be an effective church if they continued on this loveless course. They needed to return to Him to experience the continued blessing of God on their ministry. The same can happen to us. There may be time when God cuts us off from all ministry because we're having heart trouble. Yet in so doing, God reminds us that we're created for Him. He wants our hearts, not what we can do for Him. We will only experience an effective ministry as we focus on our love for Christ.

The most important and difficult task before us today as ministering women is to make more room in our hearts for God and to keep Him first. One of the ironies of ministry is that the very person who works in God's name is often hardest pressed to find time for Him. Just as the clerk in the candy store often loses his taste for candy, so the person who ministers can lose his love for God. Busy ministry, if we're not careful, can in the end become the breeding ground for the development of a cold heart toward God—a lost love.

Are you suffering today from heart trouble? Then *remember, repent* and *return again* to your First Love. For we were created to know and love Christ. The best thing in life bringing us the most joy, purpose, fulfillment, delight, and contentment is knowing and loving Christ intimately.

Oh, that we would always be First-Love Christians!

chapter five

What's Stopping You?

Overcoming six common hindrances
to the pursuit of God.

Jill Briscoe

On a typically beautiful British autumn day in 1969, my husband came cheerily into the house, joined us at the evening meal, and announced, "Well kids, we're going to America!" Our three children's eyes widened. David glanced a little nervously at his sister, who was staring into her cup.

"I know about America," David offered. "We did it in school this year."

It was true, David did know a little about America. He had been made aware of its existence through education. But awareness wasn't "knowing."

Information wasn't knowing—really knowing what America was all about. But the more we gained information, the more we began to get excited. Dad brought home baseball hats, magnets for my fridge, and a Barbie doll for Judy. But even our warm "feelings" did not constitute a true "knowing."

Knowing God, like knowing America, is much more than awareness, information, or emotional stirrings. "Knowing" is "being there." Too many of us, unfortunately, never get beyond a textbook acquaintance with God. We remain across the sea, content to base our knowledge mainly on what others describe to us. We live on our safe and comfortable islands, never exploring the vast continent, full of wonders and dangers, that waits to receive us.

What keeps us from truly experiencing God?

The Impediment of Ignorance

We often do not actively seek a deeper intimacy with God because we do not know it is possible.

The girl who led me to Christ also discipled me. I have since learned that many believers never have had a mentor or helper to holiness. We all need teachers, and if we are not in a teaching church or environment, guessing doesn't do it. We know we should read the Bible, but where do we begin, when do we do it, and how do we rightly interpret and apply what we read? Are there guidelines, rules, skills? The answer of course is yes, but guidelines need a guide, and rules and skills need to be taught. A mentor can remove so many obstacles to truly knowing and experiencing God. Sometimes we need to take the initiative and ask a wise and experienced believer to help us.

We can also learn from reading about giants of the faith. As a young believer, I inhaled biographies of men and women who knew the Lord, loved the Lord, served

"To know when to say yes or no, we also need to count the cost of our decisions. Every yes hides a no."

—Howard R. Macy—

the Lord, and were evangelistic in their zeal to make Him known. People like Hudson Taylor, C.T. Studd, Adoniram Judson, William Carey, William and Catherine Booth, Mary Slessor, and Amy Carmichael. They generously "shared" their knowledge of God with me from the pages of those books. They had been on the way a lot longer than I, and could help me adjust my sights and "go for it." These giants of the faith became mentors. The stories of men and women God has used greatly can let us into the secrets of their "knowing" and enable us to make great progress toward maturity.

The Bane of Busyness

Some of us are busy doing important things, and some of us are just busy being busy!

How busy is too busy? Who will tell me? He will! I need to learn the art of leaving things undone.

Jesus knew how to do that. One day He said to His heavenly Father, "I have brought you glory on earth by completing the work you gave me to do" (John 17:4), and went home to heaven at the age of thirty-three. Think about that. Think of all the lepers He left behind; all the hungry, maimed, blind, and demon-possessed who stayed hungry, maimed, blind, and demon-possessed because He finished the work God gave Him to do! You may be tempted to ask, how could He have finished the work that needed to be done? Oh, but it doesn't say He finished the work that needed to be done—it says He finished the work God would have Him to do. And that's why it's important to learn the secret of pleasing God! "I always do what pleases him" Jesus said (John 8:29).

The Problem of Pettiness

What is pettiness? Pettiness bothers our heads with whether we are too hot or too cold as we sit in a cushy church sanctuary; whether someone took our spot in the church parking lot, or whether anyone noticed or acknowledged our latest contribution to whatever we contributed to. Pettiness bites and devours our brothers and sisters in the Lord.

One day Jesus listened to His disciples arguing about lunch: "Open your eyes," He advised them. "Look at the fields! They are ripe for harvest" (John 4:35b). If we have our eyes fixed on the loaf of bread in our hands, we'll never see the One who grew the grain in the first place. In order that the hungry multitudes may be fed, we may find ourselves arguing which bread is best—whole wheat or white! The Lord needs to deliver us from being fascinated and captivated by our lunch. May larger hungers and the needs of a spiritually starved world lift us above the pettiness that so easily besets us.

The Lure of Laziness

Laziness is a willful decision not to go to good extremes. Our excuse for not being "spiritually disciplined" is we don't want to be called weird. We need to be balanced, laziness advises. Do a little bit of this and a little bit of that and a little bit of the other.

Laziness yawns when he hears a talk on laziness. He tunes out easily, too lazy to listen to the application. He's too lazy to concentrate on anything spiritually stretching at all, preferring drama to doctrine and music to mastering the Scriptures. He wants to be entertained, not educated. If electives are offered at church, he carefully selects ones titled, "How to Find Rest for Your Soul" or "How to Pray Effectively in Five Minutes Flat," and always arranges to work late at the office during missions festival. It's amazing how hard laziness will work to make sure he's lazy!

The Fear of the Cost

Jesus called Peter to follow Him. Peter "knew" Christ. Andrew had introduced him to the Messiah, and Peter had been hanging around Jesus in his spare time. But today was different. For Peter, this call was to leave everything and follow Jesus.

What did that mean for Peter and his family? It meant leaving his business and security, his home and environment, his trade, his independence. Peter must have feared the cost. But because he experienced the power of Christ in the miraculous catch of fish (see Luke 5:6), he fell at the Lord's feet. True, he didn't say, "take me with you," but rather, "go away from me" (Luke 5:8). But his heart was captured and his mind convinced that Jesus was Lord. When he heard the Lord's words, "Don't be afraid; from now on you will catch men," (Luke 5:10), he beached his boat and began a "knowing" God experience that he never could have had without paying a price.

There is a cost to knowing God. There has to be. Because the more you know, the more you long for others to know too. And that longing could well take you not only across the street, but perhaps even around the world!

Slaying the Sinful Self

So what in the end can keep me from coming closer to God? I can! In the final analysis, it is that sinful self—the flesh—I have been describing. My fallen nature knows how to be hostile to God without anyone telling me how. The main problem is that I don't want to be like Jesus; I want to be like me. That's the essence of the flesh. Self is all for getting, not giving; living, not dying; controlling, not releasing.

So whether it's ignorance, busyness, pettiness, laziness, or the cost, it's our innate selfishness that needs to be hammered to the cross of Christ moment by moment and day by day. Who will take the hammer and fasten me to the cross? Someone has! For as in Christ all died, so in Him will all be made alive. There it is! I can reckon myself dead indeed unto sin but alive unto God. That's a mind-set that begins in my head, then captures my heart, and finally sets my feet dancing with delight. I find that dying to self is not such a dreadful idea after all, for such a death releases me into the power and pleasure of His daily presence and delivers me from me.

chapter six

Priming Your
Devotional Life
with Hymns

Greg Asimakoupoulos

*W*hen a new Christian asks how do you keep your daily quiet time fresh and meaningful, how do you respond? What, in addition to reading a section from the Scriptures and expressing yourself to the Lord in prayer, do you do?

My mother-in-law includes a daily visit with Oswald Chambers through his classic volume, *My Utmost for His Highest*. Our friend Pete wouldn't think of maneuvering through the corporate jungle without incorporating *Our Daily Bread* into his breakfast routine. The *Covenant Home Altar* is another companion to the Bible for morning devotions. But for me a less popular book has served me well: a hymnbook.

My personal hymnal is a virtual devotional reservoir. I first discovered its artesian depth as a seminary student. A leather bound, lyric-only hymnbook caught my attention in a second-hand bookstore. Because it was only fifty cents I couldn't resist. But only after searching its yellowed pages did I realize its value had very little to do with its price tag.

Most people I know either associate the hymnal with the sanctuary of their church or with a genre of worship embraced by another generation. For me, however, the hymnal is more than a book of congregational song; it is an entire library of personal faith. The dog-eared volume beside my bed is as much at home on my nightstand as it is in the pew rack.

A Primer of Praise

My newfound old friend has taught me how to verbalize my love for God. I often struggle attempting to find words with which to express my worship. My hymnal has increased my vocabulary of praise. Reading the composer's words is like learning a new language. Imagine my joy to find these words:

Immortal, invisible
God only wise,
In light inaccessible
hid from our eyes,
Most blessed, most glorious,
the Ancient of Days
Almighty, victorious,
Thy great name we praise

or then again,

Praise to the Lord, the Almighty,
the King of creation!
O my soul, praise Him, for He is
thy health and salvation!

It is a great relief to realize my feelings of awe and joy don't have to be sentenced to silence. They could be clothed with appropriate phrases, albeit another's. With Bernard of Clairvoix I am more apt to ask "What language can I borrow to thank You dearest Friend?" And in Reginald Heber's hymn he lends me:

Holy, holy, holy!
though the darkness hides Thee,
Though the eye of sinful man
Thy glory may not see;
Only Thou are holy,
there is none beside Thee,
Perfect in power
in love and purity.

Chronicle of Confession

When I meet the Lord in quiet solitude I need to face myself before I face Him. My hymnal helps me. Within the covers of my hymnal I find me, sinful me, in the inkings of another—page after page of eloquent imperfection. Robert Robinson's lyrics mirror my life:

May Thy goodness, like a fetter,
bind my wandering heart to Thee.
Prone to wander Lord I feel it.
Prone to leave the God I love.
Here's my heart, Lord,
take and seal it,
Seal it for Thy courts above.

Mouthing those words I find myself in the company of confessors making contact with God Himself. Henry Buchnoll's verses give me courage to be candid about desires I must flee:

Break temptation's fatal power.
Shielding all with Guardian care.

Safe in every careless hour.
Safe from sloth from sensual snare.
Thou our Savior still
our failing strength repair.

It's easier to come clean with God when you have words that put it out there, plain and simple. Admitting failure in sufficient detail invites closure.

An Encyclopedia of Experience

Biographies have always been my favorite form of literature. Reading another's story gives me fresh perspective of my own story as well as windows through which to become part of theirs. My hymnal is a storybook containing countless individuals' experiences of grace. Their measured descriptions encourage me as I piggyback on their words.

When tempted to doubt the freedom Christ has won for me, I hear the prison doors clank open as I read:

Long my imprisoned spirit lay
fast bound in sin and nature's night.
Thine eye diffused a quickening ray.
I woke, the dungeon flamed with light.
My chains fell off. My heart was free.
I rose, went forth and followed Thee.

Wesley's graphic details detour my doubts. I visualize Christian's pack falling from his back in Bunyan's *Pilgrim's Progress*. I rise from my devotions able to stand less stooped.

Or when at the close of the day I question God's ability to redeem the chaos of my efforts, I am warmed by another's faith in God's father-like love.

Through many dangers, toils and snares,
I have already come.
'Tis grace that's brought me safe thus far
And grace will lead me home.

The hymn writer's admission of frustration can be just as encouraging to me as his experiences of faith. I find comfort in knowing I am not the only one who struggles with God's guidance in my life. Dora Greenwell seems guilty of reading my diary when she writes:

I am not skilled to understand
What God has willed,
what God has planned.
I only know at His right hand
is one Who is my Savior.

I, likewise, relate to the composer who chronicles his experience of discouragement as a Christian:

When I am sad at heart,
teach me Thy way.
When earthly joys depart,
teach me Thy way.
In hours of loneliness,
in times of dire distress,
In failure or success,
teach me Thy way.

A Doctrinal Diary

It was said in the sixteenth century that Martin Luther's followers sang the Reformation into being. I guess if that was the case it was because many songs within my hymnbook preach from the page. My mind is bathed in biblical truth as I begin my day with

Luther's *Ein Feste Burg*. It reminds me of God's unequaled dominion and His loving disposition toward me as revealed in His Son and Spirit.

> *And tho this world, with devils filled,*
> *should threaten to undo us,*
> *We will not fear, for God hath willed*
> *His truth to triumph thru us.*
> *The prince of darkness grim,*
> *we tremble not for him—*
> *his rage we can endure,*
> *For lo, his doom is sure:*
> *one little word shall fell him.*

> *That Word above all earthly powers,*
> *no thanks to them abideth;*
> *The Spirit and the gifts are ours*
> *thru Him who with us sideth.*
> *Let goods and kindred go,*
> *this mortal life also—*
> *the body they may kill;*
> *God's truth abideth still.*
> *His kingdom is forever.*

According to the Bible, my ability to love the One who loves me most is rooted in the Holy Spirit residing in me. George Croly's hymn describes this necessary empowerment:

> *Spirit of God,*
> *descend upon my heart;*
> *Wean it from earth,*
> *through all its pulses move;*
> *Stoop to my weakness,*
> *mighty as Thou art,*
> *And make me love Thee*
> *as I ought to love.*

More winsome than a theology text, more beautiful than a catechism, hymns are a helpful way to celebrate our beliefs as Christians. In singable sentences one after another the whole of redemption's story is told.

A Lexicon of Love

Several weeks ago a choir from Siberia performed in our church. The members of the group were not Christians. They simply wanted a place to perform while visiting America. We couldn't imagine not honoring their request. We wanted to hear their voices enunciate their new found freedom. As part of their concert of Russian folk songs and classical pieces they included a few hymns locked in vaults for over seventy years. They were awesome!

Following the program I invited the audience to stand and sing a hymn that originated in Sweden but which had passed into Russia before arriving in America. The choir, having never heard, *How Great Thou Art,* began to weep. Such a simple hymn replete with theology of creation, redemption, and heaven. The third verse contains the message of salvation in just seventy-one words.

Before the choir returned to their homeland, we presented their director with a Russian Bible and a hymnal. Nothing, in my mind, could be more appropriate to express our love and friendship. The tradition out of which I come prides itself in being people of the Book—the Bible—but my experience contends for a book in each hand that the truths they contain might live in each heart. As much as I love the refreshing informality of contemporary praise choruses, there is nothing quite like the great hymns of our faith.

Now where did you say the old family hymnal is?

chapter seven

20 Ways to Wake Up Your *Quiet Time*

Pam Farrel

ehind closed doors, many of us yawn through our quiet times. Somehow, our routine time with God slowly and quietly degenerates into a boring, predictable rut. As spiritual cataracts grow over our sleepy eyes, we may grow disinterested and frustrated. Such seasons demand a fresh view of the Creator. Like any good relationship, quiet times with God need a little variety. Instead of rolling over and hitting the snooze button, try one of these ideas for your next quiet time.

1. Write a letter to God about your life. Give it to a friend to mail back to you in three months. In the letter, talk to God about the areas of your life that are bothering you. Write about how you'd like to grow and what attribute of His you'd like to see more clearly.

2. Write out and personalize Scripture by inserting your name into promises relevant to your life or current struggles. For example, I would personalize Psalm 84:11 in this way: "No good thing does God withhold from Pam when she walks uprightly." Many of the Bible's promises come to life and seem more powerful and relevant when personalized in this way. Spend some time meditating and praying over verses that you personalize. I once copied a set of verses and strung them together as a personalized love letter from God's heart to my own. I have it framed and hanging in my room. Those personalized verses help me keep a big view of God.

3. Go on a praise walk. Thank God for everything you see. Take the opportunity to look closely at God's creation, praising Him for His creativity and the beauty of the world He's crafted. After hiking for a while, find a quiet spot to read one of the many psalms that describe His creation. Isaiah 40 and Genesis 1 are two other chapters that will help you focus your heart and mind on God's creative character.

4. Read through the Bible, mark it up, and give it as a gift to a child. If you begin early, you can plan to give the Bible as a gift to your child before an important transition, such as when he or she enters high school, leaves home, enters college, or gets married. Try to picture God through his or her eyes. With that season of life in mind, mark verses you think will help your child see and trust God in the transition to come. You might also make notes in the margin to help guide and direct the child's thinking about a passage or explain how the passage is relevant to this stage of life.

5. Spend your entire time with God singing and praising Him. Church hymnals and books of choruses are great resources to enliven your quiet time with personal worship. You might even try creating a song of your own!

6. Dance before the Lord like David, who danced "with all his might" (2 Samuel 6:14). David's dancing was a heartfelt and spontaneous expression of rejoicing. So put on your favorite hymn or praise song and dance away. Interpretive dance is a wonderful way to express your heart and soul in praise before God. If you enjoy Jewish folk dancing, ballet, or some other kind of dance, dedicate your talent to God.

7. Write down every sin that continues to haunt you. Then write 1 John 1:9 over each sin. Destroy the list—God has. This is a strong visual reminder of how God blots out your sin.

8. Write out a Philippians 4:8 list. What is lovely to you, worthy of praise, excellent, and so forth? Hang the list in a place where you tend to be grumpy, such as above the washer and dryer or on the dashboard of your car for that frustrating commute!

9. Pray in a posture you don't normally use. Try praying on your knees, prone, or standing with your face to the heavens and your hands raised in worship. It's amazing how simply changing your posture before God can change your attitude and help you experience Him in new ways.

10. Read a different translation of the Bible. You might consider purchasing a Bible that has several translations in parallel. Reading a new translation or comparing different ones can stimulate new insights into Scripture. If you've used and marked up one particular Bible for many years, reading a different Bible will enable you to see the Word with new vision. Because your eyes will not be drawn to notes and highlighted passages from previous study or devotional reading, the Scriptures will feel as beautiful and inviting as a fresh snowfall on a crisp winter morn.

11. Praise Jesus from A to Z. For example, "Jesus, You are amazing ... Jesus, You are beautiful." This activity will challenge you to think deeply about who Jesus is and why you love and serve Him. As you praise Jesus using each letter of the alphabet, spend some time meditating on each word you use to describe Him. Thinking deeply about Him is more important than racing through each letter of the alphabet as fast as you can.

> **LifeLifters**
>
> "*G*od doesn't want you busy about everything, but He does want you busy about something.
> He even knows what it is."
>
> —**Patricia H. Sprinkle**—

12. Write out your prayers to Jesus. You might write them in a journal, or purchase special stationery for these precious letters, as you might do if you were sending a letter to someone you have fallen deeply in love with. At the end of the letter, sign your name, just as you would a normal letter. Something powerful and deeply intimate happens when you record your thoughts and prayers in a letter to Jesus.

13. Make a list of the hurts and needs in your life. As you come to a verse that shows how God can meet that need, write it down next to that need. Like the letters mentioned above, you can do this in your journal or separately. You might even create a journal that records only your needs and relevant Scriptures. As you do this, you create your own book of God's promises!

14. Reread the notes of the sermon from the previous week. If your pastor is doing a series and you know what Scriptures he'll be addressing next, read ahead in the passage to be covered next Sunday. This will prepare you to think more deeply and listen better during the next sermon, as well as helping you remember and apply truth. Find a verse in the text that has helped you grow, and write a note to your pastor thanking him for his sermon and insight on the passage.

15. Read your favorite hymn. Spend some time meditating about each of the hymn's verses and its overall message. Find the passage in the Bible that the hymn was based upon, and think about how the hymn describes and reflects that truth. Spend some time researching how and why the hymn was composed. What were the circumstances? Your pastor or worship leader might know about a particular hymn's origin. Your Christian bookstore may also carry books that detail the history of certain hymns. If you're able to locate such information, think about how the hymn reflects the author's response to God during his or her circumstances.

16. Spend a period of time fasting from food, TV, or a hobby to spend more time with God. If you're able, combine your fast with a day at a quiet retreat center, the beach, the mountains, or even tucked away in a library to reflect upon God's Word and His hand in your life.

17. Have a quiet time with one of your children or grandchildren. This would probably include reading a passage from the Bible out loud. You can give children a powerful peek into your relationship with Christ by inviting them to share your regular time with God. As you ask them questions about what they see in the passage, you'll teach them to think more deeply about God's Word. Their responses and observations may surprise you, stretch you, and enrich your own perspective.

18. Write about your relationship with God from a different point of view. Think about how someone else would describe your walk. For example, my teen son might say, "My mom has a radical walk with Jesus. She really got pegged (convicted) by this verse." Several friends from the mission field explained how this activity helped them communicate the parable of the sower to the tribe they worked with. In their translation work, they described the seed that grew as the one that fell on "mulchy" soil. In that tribe, the best heart is one that resembles a compost pile. When you consider your walk and God's Word from the perspective of another, you will think differently, cross cultural barriers, and gain a fresh view of God.

19. Memorize one of the prayers of the Bible, such as Mary's prayer in Luke 1:46-55. Then act the prayer out as a soliloquy.

20. Write out a list of theological questions you'd like answered. Choose one and begin researching it. "God, what is Your heart toward women?" was a question I had that led me on an exhaustive study of all the women in the Bible, and all the verses with the words *woman* and *women* in them.

Abiding Daily

Remember, the purpose of all these ideas is to enhance your relationship with God and your intimacy with Him during your quiet time. The goal is to abide ever more in Him. As Fern Nichols, the founder of *Moms in Touch*, says, "If you seek to abide in the vine daily, you never know what day He might choose to change your life forever." Enjoy the adventure!

This article was adapted from Woman of Influence: Ten Traits of Those Who Want to Make a Difference *by Pam Farrel,* © *1996 by Pam Farrel. Used by permission of InterVarsity Press, P.O. Box 1400, Downers Grove, Illinois 60515.*

chapter eight

What's My *Story?*

Melanie M. Pruitt

"I'll never forget the difficulty I experienced several years ago when we had no money for celebrating our daughter's eighth birthday. Discontentment quickly began invading my heart."

*B*ut as I began to refocus on knowing Christ, my attitudes toward our lack of finances and possessions began to change dramatically, eventually affecting my attitude about gifts.

As it turned out, with a little creativity and renewed perspective, my daughter's birthday turned out to be one of the most memorable celebrations our family has ever had—and we had no money to spend.

Instead of buying her gifts, we decided to create a *Nutcracker* fantasy for our aspiring young ballerina.

On the morning of her birthday, Ellen was instructed to stay in her room. I served her breakfast on a tray and laid out her party clothes. Calling her Clara, her older sister helped her with her dress. When she was dressed, we started the *Nutcracker* music and Ellen entered the living room, which we had decorated. We danced together and then my husband entered, dressed as Drosselmeyer. He brought Ellen her presents from her grandparents and then we danced some more.

The night before, I had made Ellen a Clara-type nightgown; and when the music from act 1 was over, I instructed her to put it on and go to bed. This perplexed her, it being nine in the morning, but she obeyed. We quickly changed the scenery in the living room.

When we brought her out, we placed a crown on her head while we played the *Nutcracker* snow music. Then we all stood on chairs sprinkling tissue snowflakes while she danced the snowflake dance. It brought tears to my eyes as I watched her lose herself in the dance, oblivious to our presence. After the snowflake dance, we seated her in a chair designed to be a throne and each family member danced a candy dance and delivered real candies. We had a wonderful time eating chocolates and birthday cake at nine-thirty in the morning!

This birthday brought us a joy that no possession or money could have provided. This experience taught us that whenever we allow the world's ways to mix with ours we will experience discontentment. True contentment lies in a relationship ... a growing relationship with Jesus Christ who enables us to be content no matter what the circumstances—even when there is no money for a childs birthday gift!

Melanie M. Pruitt

chapter nine

Digging Deeper: *Renewing* Your Spiritual Life

... by becoming a woman of the Word

Kris Grisa

I have seen women in my small group experiences who simply can't get enough of their Bibles. They change. They grow. They are magnets in their neighborhoods and offices and people come to them in search of truth. Their families see the Bible open around the house and know that something powerful is coming to life out of those pages. These women take God delightfully seriously, and find their lives refreshed as a result. Are you one of them?

A Meditation for the Woman Who Desires the Word of God to Be Written on Her Heart.

Father in Heaven, You have surely revealed Yourself in more than one way, and I praise You for them all: this complex physical world we live in, the intellect and spirit of man himself, and, of course, the rich and deep well of revelation we call the Bible. All these reveal to us the prints of the hands that made us.

If it weren't for Your willingness to show us and tell us what You are like, we would be lost and confused in this world. Without the commands and assurances in Your Word, I would be in the dark about who I am and what I should be doing in this world. But with Your Word impressed on my heart, I am able to be a living revelation of You. Jesus, the Word, help me take my relationship with Your Word more seriously.

Ask Yourself These Questions Before You Continue ...

• Does God's Word have the place of prominence in my life that it deserves?

• How do I demonstrate this, aside from my personal reading of the Word (in the areas of Scripture memory, use of the Word in giving counsel, meditation, teaching my children)?

• How would my life look different if I placed higher regard on the power of the Word (in the areas of sin management, evangelism, wisdom, intimacy with my Father, in my priorities)?

In speech I testify to the power of Your Word, Jesus, but in my heart I don't see the connection that should be evident. I confess my casual affection for the words of life that You have been so faithful to pass to us in the Scriptures. My study and my meditations are "on again, off again" according to my schedule and mood; but, I have seen the sharpness of Your two-edged sword pierce both my and others' souls by its awesome truth telling. You've been faithful to comfort, instruct, rebuke, and train me by Your Word, and I thank You for those experiences. Cleanse me of the sin of pride that sneaks in quietly lest I find myself thinking I can live successfully without You ministering to me through Your Word.

Search Yourself Again Through Confession (Let the Ten Commandments Be Your Guide):

• Do I know of an area where I'm out of line with God's Word in my thought life (covetousness, dishonoring attitude toward my spouse, idolatry)?

• Am I out of line with one of His commandments in my public life (keeping a Sabbath, honoring my parents, some form of stealing or deceit)?

• Am I out of line in some area because it is too costly to change?

Make the Following Your Prayer:

"I have strayed like a lost sheep. Seek Your servant, for I have not forgotten Your commands." Your Word is my lamp, Holy One. It searches out my inner life and also guides my outward steps toward obedience. Keep this tough ministry to me alive and useful, even though I must face the disheartening reality of my sin. Never let me shy away from the brightness of Your light, trying to protect my areas of sin—those places that You would transform into godliness and use to reveal truth to others. "Direct my footsteps according to Your Word; let no sin rule over me."

Make me a woman of integrity whose thoughts are as monitored by Your commands as are my actions. Keep me from the easy sin of hypocrisy. May my family, my inner circle, and You who see my hidden heart, all know me to be the same woman the rest of the world sees. I need the absoluteness of Your truth to set my boundaries. I humbly ask for insight to understand more deeply what I read in the Bible. I want what You want for me: the profound intimacy and awe for You that would make my heart melt and open to anything and everything You would say to me. "My flesh trembles in fear of You; I stand in awe of Your laws." "Open my eyes that I may see wonderful things in Your law."

> ### Life Lifters
>
> "*My* goal is God Himself, not joy nor peace, nor even blessing, but Himself, my God."
>
> —**Oswald Chambers**—

In closing your devotional time, give thought to those whom you study the Word of God with. Name each one of them before God in prayer and thank Him for how He uses you in their lives. Pray for the integrity of your study times together — that His truth would be handled correctly. Pray for change in each other's lives as the truth reaches its mark in each heart. Pray for your community impact—that your application of the Word would reach beyond your group to accomplish the work God has for you.

May it be, Lord, that I can say, after the words of Jeremiah 31, that I am a woman called according to Your ancient but current covenant, and that You are putting Your law in my mind, not just in a book of words which I read; and that You are writing Your law on my heart so that I can be counted among those that say they "Know the Lord!" Amen.

chapter ten

Counseling Corner:
A Friend Loves at All Times

Ingrid Lawrenz, MSW

For years I had enjoyed Mary's friendship. We had fun laughing and being kind of crazy together. I could count on her for an understanding empathy and a challenging discussion. We could get into a conflict and disagree without fear of lasting negative consequences. Our small children jumped at any excuse to get together. But right now I dreaded going to see her. My stomach was sick. Excuses of other important things to do flew through my mind. Yet a deeper value, a commitment of my heart and mind, made me go. She was my friend and I loved her and that was that!

At this point she had maybe a month or two left to live. She was dying before my eyes as cancer ravaged her body. She was thirty-two years old. Her vitality, authenticity, and exuberance flickered like a lamp running out of oil. It hurt so much to see her, but because of my empathy for her I had to remind myself that it was not I who was dying and leaving my children. God had not asked that of me (at least not yet), but He had asked me to love Mary at all times even though I wanted nothing more than to go into denial and run.

I remember shortly before she died being at a young couple's retreat together, where I, like all good ministry wives, was speaking. At one point I had to run to my own room in order to collapse in uncontrolled sobbing, repeating over and over to God, "But she's my friend." The shame I felt for not being able to help ease her pain was incapacitating. How could I go and lead a seminar? Months later, after her death, I faced a similar question: how can I stand up at her funeral and give a testimony of her life? Somehow I took comfort in C.S. Lewis's words that "if you give your heart to anything, even a pet, in this world you will be hurt, because the only place you can go not to be hurt by love is hell, because in hell there is no love."

I framed a Favia card in my office that says, "Some people come into your life and quickly go, others come in and leave footprints and you are never ever the same." My life has changed because of my friendship with Mary. I believe I will be braver and more courageous about facing my own death due to her model. I see the value of the depth of love and richness in life that comes from being honest with and fully experiencing all of our emotions. Of letting others in close enough to see them and therefore feeling connected with these friends and not so alone. Even during the darkest weeks, Mary had a way of expressing love, gratitude, or encouragement to me. She was able to give and receive love—this is what friendship is all about. Proverbs 17:17 says, "A friend loves at all times."

I heard a talk about burnout in ministry in which the speaker said that ministry people tend to have an abundance of *drainers* and *neutrals* in their lives. Neutrals are people we rub shoulders with regularly but who neither take from nor give to us. The speaker went on to say, "We need to make sure we also have friends in our lives who are replenishers." Replenishers are mutuals, allies in battle. We can be real with them and relaxed. The laughter, the stimulating discussions, the empathetic understanding, leaves us feeling somehow *fuller* than we were.

> ### Life Lifters
> "*P*ut first things first and we get second things thrown in; put second things first and we lose both first and second things."
> —**C.S. Lewis**—

As ministry wives, we need a variety of replenishing friends in our lives in order to have the energy, compassion, and endurance to have a bucket that never runs dry as we pour our lives out to others for Christ's sake. As a therapist, I remind my clients—and also myself, which is often the way it goes in counseling—that they need support from a number of people in order to cope and keep running the race. Putting *all your eggs in one basket*, so to speak, is dangerous. One person can't always be there and our needs and interests are so numerous that spreading them out over a *support network* is very helpful. While I believe our spouse should be our closest confidante and best friend—a bond that no one else enters into— we need other friends, especially of the same sex.

As is often the case in ministry, there are times when we are both so burdened down—as we were with Mary's illness and death—that we didn't have much left for each other, so we needed to lean on others. Or there are times when your husband just doesn't understand—be it PMS or your passion for gardening—that another female friend can really connect with.

Since there are many facets of your life, it is helpful to find a variety of friends. Some times you connect on just one facet—on ministry issues for example—as with another ministry wife, while another friend crosses three or four issues, perhaps: emotional connectedness, common hobbies, or mothering issues. It really is okay to have friends in different orbits of closeness like the planets to the sun. It is nice to have a *best friend* or *closest friend* (but they aren't always easy to find). And even if we do have a special friend, we need others to keep us from expecting too much from that one person. I am saddened to hear my clients minimize or denigrate as unimportant the friends they have who cross only one or two facets of their lives. Too often they are looking for the *perfect parent* in a friend to meet all their needs instead of appreciating and enjoying the support, mutuality, and interest of the different people in different orbits in their lives.

The same weekend Mary died, I received the news of a close friend's deception to me concerning long-term immorality. I was devastated to say the least. It could have been a time to pull in, shut down, or stop trusting. Fortunately for me as a professional counselor, I've seen enough people choose that route only to die inside—growing cold to God and despairing—"the only place you can go to not be hurt by love is hell, because in hell there is no love." At that time, I found friendships in people who had been there all along but somehow the bridge had never been crossed before. I found deeper friendship in the common hurt, but mutual support we fellow mourners shared. Jesus also valued His friends and didn't deem it necessary to "go it alone with God the Father."

I gladly cherish the gifts God has given to me in mutual friends, and pray that I will be a good "replenishing" friend to others, even the drainers in my life. If God in fact *is love*, I pray that His love will radiate to and through me in all of my relationships.

chapter eleven

Mentoring Moments—
Can Peers be
Mentors?

Win Couchman

For eleven years I have been an enthusiastic participant of a peer-mentoring group. Four women meet once a month to listen to and pray for each other. The group has surprised me with joy. We are peers in spiritual commitment rather than age, for the other three women in the group are a generation younger than I. We are mentors in an unplanned but highly significant sense. As we listen to one another share about the past month, we learn how she has managed with God's help. Her imperfect, but eager, Christianity helps the rest of us as we listen. So, without realizing it, each in turn mentors the others.

More specifics about how our group works are listed below, but here are some general aspects:

• The group works because we are spiritually at about the same place. In other groups we are involved with, we disciple or lead. This is a group where equals encourage each other.

• We trust one another, so we don't need to be concerned about keeping confidences.

- Month after month, the three who arrive at my house throw themselves into chairs and blurt out: "I'm so glad to be here!" This sense of relief comes, I think, because we all feel safe enough to really relax.

- The purpose of the group is to encourage and strengthen one another by careful listening and prayer. It is a luxury to talk out our month with women who love us. The stories we share are simply the stories of what happened in us and to us since we last met.

LifeLifters

"*Love* the Lord your God with all your heart and with all your soul and with all your strength."

—Deuteronomy 6:5—

Why be part of such a group? To know I am loved, prayed over, listened to, and appreciated by the same women for so long has made me willing to share openly my own areas of immaturity, anxiety, and other places where I need to change. God is using these women to complete His work in me.

How Does Peer Mentoring Work?

1. We limited our group to four, because only four stories will fit into one evening!

2. Meeting only once a month is ideal for busy women.

3. We are not all from the same church or social circles. That is helpful, but not essential.

We are not a *secret* group, but neither do we tell other people what takes place when we meet. Because we don't often see each other between meetings, we don't need to be careful about what we say in other settings.

4.   An intentional part of our evenings is to keep all of our comments on holy ground—to be aware of God's presence, to seek Him in all that is said and done.

5.   Toward this end, we always begin with worship. Someone brings a Bible passage that has been meaningful to her, and we read, discuss, and pray. This sets the tone for our times together. Almost always, the passage we study throws light on a struggle, question, or a blessing that comes up in our sharing time. God does that.

6.   Prayer notebooks are the journals in which we record prayer requests, praises, and mini-schedules for the coming month. Three of us busily write while the fourth woman tells us what has been happening, and adds what she expects will take place in the coming month, asking us for prayer or sharing praises. Often we stop and pray for a woman right as she is speaking. Sometimes, we even find ourselves weeping with each other, and now and then a deep and restful silence settles over us as we sense God's presence. Other times, we laugh so hard that we nearly fall off our chairs, as we share the ridiculous or the comical in our lives.

7.   We have coffee and *something*. The *something* may be frozen yogurt or an elaborate pastry picked up on someone's way to the group. Anything is appreciated, but the treats do not dominate our precious time.

8.   The group has become a place of great safety, where truth is foundational and kindness characteristic. We are able to bear repeated prayer needs. We are sisters in Christ.

Author Biographies

Jill Briscoe is a popular writer and conference speaker who has authored over forty books. She directs Telling the Truth media ministries with her husband, Stuart, and ministers through speaking engagements around the world. Jill is executive editor of *Just Between Us*, a magazine for ministry wives and women in leadership, and serves on the boards of World Relief and Christianity Today International. Jill and Stuart live in suburban Milwaukee, Wisconsin, and have three grown children and thirteen grandchildren.

Lonnie Collins Pratt has published over 500 articles and is a frequent conference speaker. Lonnie is a voracious reader, consuming more than 200 books a year. She lives in Lapeer, Michigan.

Ingrid Lawrenz, MSW is a licensed social worker who has been counseling for seventeen years. Ingrid has been a pastor's wife for twenty-seven years and is currently the senior pastor's wife at Elmbrook Church in Brookfield, Wisconsin. She and her husband, Mel, have two teenagers and live in Waukesha, Wisconsin.

Shelly Esser has been the editor of *Just Between Us*, a magazine for ministry wives and women in leadership, for the last thirteen years. She has written numerous published articles and ministered to women for over twenty years. Her recent book, *My Cup Overflows—A Deeper Study of Psalm 23* encourages women to discover God's shepherd love and care for them. She lives in southeastern Wisconsin, with her husband, John, and four daughters.

author biographies

Greg Asimakoupoulos is an ordained minister and freelance writer. His articles have appeared regularly in a variety of Christian periodicals. Greg has also authored several books including, *The Time Crunch, Jesus, the People's Choice, Prayers from My Pencil,* and *Heroic Faith.* Greg and his wife, Wendy, have three daughters and live in Naperville, Illinois.

Pam Farrel is director of women's ministries at Valley Bible Church in San Marcos, California. A pastor's wife and the mother of three, she has been discipling women for over fifteen years. A seasoned writer, she has authored over sixteen books in addition to hosting a radio show. She and her husband, Bill, co-direct Masterful Living, an organization to encourage today's marriages and families.

Melanie M. Pruitt is a pastor's wife in Washougal, Washington. Melanie is a freelance author and speaker for women's retreats, workshops, and conferences. She and her husband, Bill, provide premarital counseling for engaged couples, and Melanie is involved in discipleship with the women of her church. She and her husband have three children.

Kris Grisa has spent many years involved in small group leadership. She is an avid disciple maker, teaching women and girls in small group settings through her local church. Kris is also a writer of devotional materials. She and her husband, John, live in Brookfield, Wisconsin, with their three children.

–61–

Win Couchman has spent much of her life ministering as a bible teacher, speaker, writer, and counselor. She and her husband, Bob, also served as missionaries with International Teams and as lay leaders in their church for many years. Win's life is flowing over at the top as she is fully engaged in life. She and her husband live in Menomonee Falls, Wisconsin.

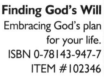

Prayer that Works
Plugging into the
power source.
ISBN 0-78143-953-1
ITEM #102352

Only
$5.99
each!

Resolving Conflict
Stilling the storms of life.
ISBN 0-78143-954-X
ITEM #102353

The Search for Balance
Keeping first things first.
ISBN 0-78143-955-8
ITEM #102354

Spiritual Warfare
Equipping yourself for battle.
ISBN 0-78143-948-5
ITEM #102347

**To get these excellent resources, visit us online at
www.cookministries.com or call 1-800-323-7543!**